Uncaged Hearts and Flying Dreams

Hearts unfurl like wings in spring,
Chasing hopes that gently sing.
With every breath, the spirit soars,
Breaking free from hidden doors.

Encased in light, they dance and twirl,
Painting skies, they freely swirl.
In open fields, they find their way,
Embracing life in bright array.

Echoes in the Rearview

Whispers linger in the night,
Memories wrapped in soft twilight.
Shadows stretch and fade away,
Carried forth on winds of gray.

Reflections dance on glassy streets,
Time retreats, yet never ceases.
Every glance, a story told,
Fragments lost and dreams of old.

The Weight of Forgotten Dreams

Heavy lies the heart in shade,
Restless echoes slowly fade.
In the dark, aspirations sigh,
Buried deep, they yearn to fly.

The dreams we held now gather dust,
In silent corners, they adjust.
Yet still they beckon, softly gleam,
Awakening the quiet dream.

Unpacking Memories

Boxes filled with faded letters,
Time-worn tales and gentle fetters.
Each artifact a secret kiss,
Reminding us of love's abyss.

Memories wrapped in fragile lace,
Transport us to that cherished place.
With every layer, feelings bloom,
Unpacking joy, dispelling gloom.

Pieces of a Broken History

Shattered dreams lay in the dust,
Whispers of lives once lived,
Fragments clung to ancient walls,
Echoes of the past still give.

Reflections on Water's Edge

Ripples dance on the surface,
Mirrored skies above me fade,
Silhouettes of time and place,
In the stillness, memories wade.

The Road Ahead Beckons

Footsteps light on untraveled paths,
Sunrise spills gold on the way,
Horizon calls with sweet promises,
Adventure waits, come what may.

Unraveling Old Stories

Pages worn with years of hands,
Tales of love and heartache blend,
Voices linger, shadows dance,
In each word, lives never end.

When Tomorrow's Light Breaks Through

In the hush of night's embrace,
A whisper stirs the dawn.
Dreams fade like morning mist,
As new hopes are reborn.

With colors bold, the sun will rise,
Casting shadows long and deep.
Each moment, a chance to realign,
Awakening those who sleep.

The sky ignites in shades of gold,
As darkness takes its flight.
Promise dances on the breeze,
When tomorrow's light breaks bright.

Each heartbeat pulses with the day,
Renewed strength to carry on.
The past is but a fading song,
Now the future beckons strong.

So let your spirit break the chains,
And soar beyond the blue.
With every step, reclaim your path,
When tomorrow's light breaks through.

Pages Turned, Stories Untold

A book lays open on the shelf,
Dust gathers on each page.
Chapters filled with dreams and fears,
Of love and bitter rage.

Each word a breath, a heartbeat shared,
In the twilight of our mind.
Stories linger in the silence,
Awaiting to be aligned.

With every turn, a world unfolds,
Adventure awaits the brave.
We write our fate with ink and hope,
In the tales we dare to save.

Memories like whispers chase,
The shadows of our soul.
Pages turned reveal the paths,
We've walked, both kind and whole.

So pen your thoughts with open heart,
Let your stories take their toll.
For in the end, we are the words,
Of pages turned, stories told.

Seeds of Change in the Heart's Garden

In the depths of quiet earth,
Lie the seeds of what may be.
Whispers of a brighter dawn,
Awaiting to break free.

With patience, we will tend the soil,
And nurture dreams with care.
Watered by our hopes and tears,
The bloom we long to share.

Beneath the surface, life stirs on,
In shadows, growth takes place.
The heart's garden holds the promise,
Of blossoms full of grace.

As seasons shift, the winds will blow,
Change dances through the air.
Each petal tells a story new,
Of love, of joy, of dare.

Let us plant with faith and trust,
In the garden of our soul.
For seeds of change will always grow,
When we believe in whole.

A Final Dance with Ghosts

In the twilight of our dreams,
Shadows waltz and sway.
Echoes of the life we had,
Haunting every day.

Whispers float upon the breeze,
Stories left behind.
Memories, a fragile thread,
In the labyrinth of the mind.

We twirl among the memories,
Each step a bittersweet song.
In the silence, they remind us,
Of the places we belong.

With every heartbeat, they draw near,
Glimmers of faded light.
A final dance with ghosts we know,
As we say our last goodnight.

So hold their essence in your heart,
Let love never be lost.
For every dance, we once shared here,
Is worth the aching cost.

The Last Train to Tomorrow

The whistle shrieks through the night,
A beckoning call to the future's light.
Ghostly shadows dance on the track,
As dreams whisper where the past won't go.

Metal wheels grind, a steady beat,
Carrying hopes wrapped up in heat.
Passengers clutch their stories tight,
As dawn breaks forth, chasing the night.

Fires of yesterday flicker and fade,
In the cold of a morning that won't evade.
Yet in the distance, the horizon gleams,
The last train whispers of tomorrow's dreams.

Through the fog, the engines roar,
Rumbling softly like love's implore.
With every mile, fears are shed,
Onboard this journey, look ahead.

The journey's end is yet to be told,
In future's embrace, watch the brave unfold.
So leap aboard while time still flows,
The last train to tomorrow gently goes.

Bellows of Change in the Stillness

In silent woods where whispers sway,
The change unfurls in quiet display.
Leaves flutter soft like secrets shared,
Under the night, the world prepared.

A haunting song breaks through the calm,
Rising like the breath of a balm.
Echoes of life, they twist and twine,
Bellows of change in the still, divine.

Stars blink down on a velvet sea,
Reflecting dreams of what might be.
Each flicker, a whisper, a wish to blend,
In the dance of shadows, where hopes ascend.

With every heartbeat, nature calls,
Change wraps around as silence falls.
Embrace the shift, let old depart,
For in the stillness, lies a new start.

So linger in dreams under moon's soft glow,
Invite the changes, let your spirit flow.
With every breath, the world rearranges,
In deep, silent woods, bellows of changes.

Breaching the Veil of Regret

In the quiet hours of night's embrace,
Regret drapes softly, a whispered lace.
Choices made like shadows loom,
Treading lightly in the silent room.

Faces flash like fleeting lights,
Memories echo in lonely nights.
Yearning hearts seek peace in pain,
Breaching the veil where truth remains.

A mirror reflects the battles fought,
Lessons learned but never caught.
In the dance of loss, we find the grace,
As regrets fade, they leave no trace.

Forgive the echoes; let them be,
Weightless thoughts set the spirit free.
For in acceptance, lies the key,
Breaching the veil to set us free.

So walk through shadows, find the dawn,
In the light where past is gone.
With each step, we learn to forget,
In the journey forward, breaching regret.

A Quiet Release from Yesterday

As daylight breaks, the shadows flee,
A gentle breath of certainty.
The weight of time begins to lift,
And in its wake, the heart finds gift.

Echoes of yesterday ring so faint,
In the silence blooms a little saint.
With tender hands, the past unspools,
Each thread woven in shining jewels.

The winding path leads to the dawn,
With every step, the fear is gone.
A quiet release in the morning's song,
Where the soul knows it still belongs.

As petals fall from the tired bloom,
Acknowledge light, release the gloom.
Embrace the dawn with open arms,
For in this moment, lie all charms.

So softly hum a whispered grace,
To find tomorrow in a warm embrace.
In quiet release, let shadows play,
For each new day brings light to stay.

Embracing the Unfamiliar

In shadows deep, a path unfolds,
Where whispers call, and courage molds.
Each step taken, a heartbeat near,
New worlds await, dissolve the fear.

Through tangled vines, we forge ahead,
With open hearts, where dreams are spread.
The unknown beckons, wild and free,
In every turn, a chance to see.

With every heartbeat, doubts may wane,
In silence deep, we learn the gain.
Unfamiliar songs begin to play,
And guide us gently through the fray.

So take the leap, and trust the fall,
For in the dark, you hear the call.
Embrace the wild, let shadows blend,
And find the light that leads to mend.

Navigating the New Dawn

As night retreats, the sky turns gold,
Each breath we take, a story told.
The morning light, a gentle song,
With every step, we find where we belong.

The horizon opens, vast and bright,
In every heart, a spark of light.
We sail through clouds, on winds so fair,
As whispered dreams drift through the air.

With eyes wide open, we chase the sun,
In all its warmth, our fears are done.
Each moment born, a gift anew,
Together we rise, like morning dew.

So let us journey, side by side,
With hope to guide us through the tide.
Navigating paths, both bold and true,
In the embrace of a world anew.

The Solace of New Beginnings

In quiet corners, new dreams grow,
The seeds we plant begin to flow.
With open palms and lifted eyes,
We greet the dawn, where wonder lies.

Each heartbeat sings, a song of grace,
In every challenge, we find our place.
The dawn reminds us, fresh and clear,
That change can bloom, dispel the fear.

With every ending, a chance to start,
New hues of hope paint every heart.
In gentle whispers, courage wakes,
Embracing love, for our own sakes.

So let the past dissolve like mist,
In every moment, dreams persist.
The solace found in paths untried,
Is where our spirits soar and glide.

Unseen Twists of Fate

In the labyrinth of time we roam,
Through hidden paths, we find our home.
The threads of life weave stories rare,
In unexpected turns, we share.

A glance, a smile, a fateful meet,
The dance of chance beneath our feet.
With every choice, the map unfolds,
Where destinies are brave and bold.

In jumbled steps, new chances rise,
To guide us through the boundless skies.
In every stumble, lessons gained,
The beauty found when we are strained.

So trust the winds to shift your fate,
Embrace the dance, don't hesitate.
For in the unknown, joy awaits,
In unseen twists, ignite your stakes.

The Canvas of Tomorrow

Brushstrokes of dreams across the sky,
Colors of hope, we let them fly.
Every heartbeat a vibrant hue,
A masterpiece made by me and you.

In the morning light, visions unfold,
Stories of courage, whispered bold.
With each sunrise, a chance to create,
A future a-paint, it's never too late.

Whispers of change in the gentle breeze,
A canvas awaits, eager to please.
Strokes of our laughter, splashes of tears,
Every detail etched through the years.

Together we build, together we dream,
Each tiny moment, a flowing stream.
In the realm of tomorrow, we take our stand,
With brushes in hand, let's paint the land.

Unfurling New Horizons

The dawn breaks gently, colors ignite,
Shadows retreat, giving way to light.
With every step, we chase our fate,
Horizons expand, we can't wait.

Mountains behind us, valleys ahead,
Whispers of possibility, softly said.
As dreams take shape, we learn to soar,
With hearts wide open, we seek for more.

In the distance, new worlds arise,
Serenading our souls, under vast skies.
Together we rise, as time unfurls,
Uncharted paths lead to new worlds.

Hands joined in trust, we venture forth,
Every journey a quest of worth.
With spirit and courage, we'll reach our prize,
New horizons beckon, oh how they rise.

When Roots Turn to Wings

In the heart of the earth, we find our place,
Nurtured by love, surrounded by grace.
From stillness we grow, deep down we dig,
When roots turn to wings, oh how we big!

Tender shoots reaching for the sun,
Each little struggle, a story begun.
Breaking the soil, embracing the light,
Transforming our fears into wondrous flight.

The strength that we gather from darkened days,
Becomes a foundation in myriad ways.
With every leap, we rise above,
Embodied in courage, anchored in love.

So spread out your wings, let darkness fall,
Explore the vast realms, heed the call.
When roots turn to wings, we are free,
To dance with the wind, to simply be.

Cycles of Change

Seasons whisper soft on the breeze,
Painting the world with such gentle ease.
Leaves turn to gold, then fall to rest,
Each moment a lesson, a subtle quest.

Time turns like pages in a worn book,
Every chapter reveals, if we only look.
With each cycle, we learn to bend,
Finding strength in change, our eternal friend.

The river flows onward, carving its way,
Teaching us patience, come what may.
In shadows and sunlight, growth intertwines,
Cycles of change, like ancient rhymes.

Embrace the twists, the turns, the flows,
Life's fragile beauty in each ebb and rose.
For in every ending, a beginning starts,
A rhythm of life that connects our hearts.

Horizons Beyond Blue

Endless skies stretch far and wide,
Whispers of dreams in the evening tide.
Mountains rise where hopes take flight,
Stars awaken in the soft twilight.

Waves crash gently on the shore,
Each moment sings of something more.
Birds on the wing, in graceful dance,
Guide the heart in a timeless trance.

Colors blend in a vibrant hue,
Painting life in shades anew.
The sun dips low, a fiery glow,
Awakens wonder in shadows below.

Paths await with secrets untold,
As journeys unfold, we grow bold.
With every step, the world expands,
Horizons change as we understand.

In the silence, dreams ignite,
Every whisper a spark of light.
Beyond the blue, our spirits soar,
Finding treasures on the vibrant shore.

The Gallery of Forgotten Dreams

In silent halls where shadows creep,
Lies a tapestry of dreams we keep.
Framed in dust, they wait in line,
Whispers of hopes once thought divine.

Canvas of wishes, brushed with grace,
Faded colors in time's embrace.
Each stroke a tale, each tear a sigh,
Memories woven in the gallery's eye.

Voices echo in the quiet night,
Calling forth the lost delight.
Portraits linger with stories true,
Every frame a piece of you.

Some dreams are buried, some shine bright,
In the gallery's glow, they find their light.
A dance of ghosts, a rhythm so sweet,
In the heart's chamber, they repeat.

Unveiling the past, we dare to see,
The beauty in each missed decree.
With every glance, the soul redeems,
In the gallery of forgotten dreams.

Chasing the Horizon

Feet on the ground, hearts in the air,
Chasing the light, we follow the flare.
The horizon calls, a siren's song,
A path unknown where we belong.

Clouds drift by in hues of gold,
Stories whisper of the brave and bold.
Each step we take is a dance of fate,
In the chase of dreams, we recreate.

Mountains rise, valleys deep,
In this journey, memories we keep.
The sun sets low, casting its glow,
Guiding our hearts where love can flow.

Through fields of wildflowers we roam,
Finding in nature our truest home.
With every dawn, a brand new day,
Chasing horizons that light the way.

The journey is long, but spirits high,
In the chase of dreams, we reach for the sky.
The horizon beckons with open arms,
Inviting us all to its endless charms.

The Art of Moving Forward

With the dawn comes a fresh new start,
Life's canvas waits for the brush of heart.
Colors blend in the morning light,
Creating visions, pure and bright.

Steps may falter on unsteady ground,
But courage rises, a strength profound.
In the face of doubt, we learn to stand,
Crafting a future, with hopeful hands.

Each scar we bear tells a story bold,
Of battles fought and dreams retold.
Through shadows cast, we find our way,
The art of moving forward, day by day.

Embracing change, we shed the past,
In the river of time, we flow steadfast.
With every heartbeat, we write our tale,
In the art of life, we shall prevail.

So here we rise, like the sun's first beam,
Building a world that holds our dream.
With every stroke, we pave the path,
In the art of moving, we find our math.

The Transformation of Worn-Out Wings

Once they were tattered, frayed at the seam,
A testament to battles and lost dreams.
Now they shimmer, catching the light,
Ready to soar, embracing the night.

Each feather sings tales of skies once crossed,
Of hopes reborn and friendships lost.
In the silence of dusk, they whisper clear,
A new flight awaits, with nothing to fear.

From ashes of doubt, they lift and rise,
To dance with the stars, where freedom lies.
No longer bound by the weight of the past,
They find in their strength, a future vast.

So let them take wing, these hearts made whole,
In the warmth of the sun, they reclaim their soul.
For every worn-out wing has a story to tell,
A journey of healing, of breaking the shell.

Now they embrace the winds of change,
Transforming their fate, no longer strange.
The world below fades, a distant thing,
As they learn to trust in the power of wing.

Shattered Chains of Histories

Chains once clinked, a haunting sound,
Echoes of sorrow that lingered around.
Each link a story, heavy with pain,
Now whispered away in a gentle rain.

The past, a shadow, looms in the mist,
Yet courage finds ways to quietly resist.
With every break, a piece of the weight,
The heart gives in to the rhythms of fate.

From ashes of chains, a phoenix will rise,
Unveiling the strength that within us lies.
No longer confined by what used to be,
Embracing a vision, we begin to see.

We walk through the fire, the heat we endure,
Emerging as one, united and pure.
The shattered remains scatter on the ground,
A testament to freedom, finally found.

With every step forward, we leave the dark,
Illuminated paths, igniting a spark.
Together we rise, as history fades,
In the light of tomorrow, our hope cascades.

Eclipsing the Shadows of Old Journeys

Old journeys linger, shadows stretch long,
Hushed whispers of where we once belonged.
Yet in this twilight, a new dawn unfolds,
With stories untold, and futures bold.

We carry our burdens, but not on our backs,
The weight of the past no longer distracts.
Each step in the light, a choice to be made,
Turning the page, letting moments cascade.

Eclipsing the shadows, we rise to the call,
With every heartbeat, we shatter the wall.
Finding the strength in the lessons we've learned,
Transforming the pain into flames that have burned.

The path may be winding, with turns unknown,
Yet in every heartbeat, we'll find our own tone.
With courage as compass, we navigate right,
Illuminated hearts guide us into the night.

Together we'll journey, wherever it leads,
Through valleys of doubt or the crown of the reeds.
For eclipsing our shadows is merely the start,
A dance of the brave, a song of the heart.

Unfurling the Map to Tomorrow

Amidst the whispers of an ancient shore,
Lies a map unfolding, with tales of yore.
Each line a promise, each mark a dream,
A journey awaits, igniting the theme.

With colors of hope, it paints the sky,
Guiding the lost, urging them to fly.
Through mountains of courage, through rivers of grace,
The path to tomorrow, we boldly embrace.

In the fabric of now, we weave our fate,
Threads of resilience, never too late.
A canvas of wishes, where visions ignite,
With the spark of tomorrow, we dance in the light.

So gather your dreams, let the world know,
The future's a river, a radiant flow.
Unfurling the map, with every wise move,
We shape our own fate, as hearts begin to groove.

In moments we'll cherish, with laughter and tears,
Together we journey, dispelling our fears.
For the map to tomorrow is drawn with our souls,
A masterpiece crafted, where each heart consoles.

Embracing the Unwritten Tomorrow

A dawn breaks soft and light,
With dreams that spark and soar,
Each heartbeat whispers hope,
And opens every door.

Unfolding paths await,
With courage in our hands,
We step into the unknown,
Where destiny expands.

Moments weave like thread,
In tapestry divine,
We paint our visions bright,
With colors bold, we shine.

Fear melts like morning frost,
With every breath we take,
We rise, we learn, we grow,
Our hearts will never break.

So let's embrace the dawn,
With every whispered prayer,
The future's ours to mold,
With love, we will declare.

Wings of Change on the Horizon

The sky dances in hues,
Of orange, pink, and gray,
A whisper of the winds,
That beckons us to play.

Change stirs like gentle waves,
Transforming what we know,
With every rise and fall,
A chance for us to grow.

The sun sets, shadows stretch,
Yet hope remains aglow,
With courage in our souls,
We let our spirits flow.

The horizon calls our names,
With promise in its reach,
We spread our wings and fly,
Embracing all we teach.

For in the winds of time,
New paths will always form,
With love and faith combined,
We'll face the coming storm.

Reflections in a Broken Mirror

Fragments scatter light,
Shards of dreams once whole,
We piece them back with care,
To reveal a deeper soul.

What once was clear and bright,
Now dances in disguise,
The beauty in the cracks,
Holds secrets, truths, and lies.

We learn to face the flaws,
With courage in our gaze,
Each fracture tells a tale,
Of love in all its ways.

Through broken images,
We glimpse a hidden grace,
Embracing every edge,
In this imperfect space.

So let the mirror shine,
Reflecting all we find,
For in our brokenness,
Our hearts are reassigned.

Whispered Goodbyes in the Wind

The leaves rustle softly,
As daylight starts to fade,
We gather our sweet thoughts,
In memories displayed.

With every breath we share,
A piece of us remains,
In laughter, in the tears,
Through losses and through gains.

Goodbyes whisper like waves,
Crashing on the shore,
Yet in each ebb and flow,
Love lingers evermore.

The wind carries our words,
To places far and wide,
Where echoes of our hearts,
In silence still abide.

So as we part, remember,
The bond we cannot sever,
In every whispered goodbye,
Love's thread lasts forever.

Dissonance of the Past

Echoes linger in the night,
Whispers of forgotten plight.
Shadows dance on fragile dreams,
Time unravels at the seams.

Faded pictures on the wall,
Silent screams, an unheard call.
History's weight, a heavy chain,
Lessons lost, but etched in pain.

Memories draped in shades of gray,
Moments lost along the way.
Sights once clear now blurred and faint,
A haunting tune, a ghostly saint.

Fragments of a life once lived,
A past that haunts yet won't forgive.
In the silence, truths reside,
Dissonance that won't subside.

New Roads and New Skies

Beneath a canvas vast and wide,
New horizons call with pride.
Each step forward, fresh and bold,
Stories waiting to be told.

Winding paths stretch far ahead,
With every heartbeat, life is fed.
Mountains high and rivers deep,
Promises in every leap.

Winds of change, a gentle guide,
In the journey, love abides.
Clouds may gather but won't stay,
Sunshine breaks with each new day.

Fields of gold beneath our feet,
Every moment bittersweet.
The road ahead, a grand surprise,
Life unfolds 'neath endless skies.

Unfading Directions

Stars above, a map of fate,
Guiding hearts that hesitate.
Through the maze of night and light,
Hope will always lead us right.

Voices echo, soft yet clear,
Whispers that we long to hear.
Paths diverge but always meet,
In every challenge, we find our feet.

Unfading dreams will spark the flame,
Fueling souls, igniting names.
Together we will find our ways,
In the art of living days.

With each turn, new lessons learned,
In the fire, the heart has burned.
As we wander, we grow wise,
Following the unfading skies.

Beneath the Weight of Memory

Memories stack like ancient stone,
Carried burdens of the known.
Every joy and every pain,
Marks our path, leaves its stain.

Beneath the weight, we stand so still,
Time's embrace, a bitter thrill.
Yesterday's laughter, tomorrow's tears,
Reflections shimmer through the years.

Yet within the quiet dusk,
Lives a promise, a whispered trust.
In every shadow lies the light,
Guiding us to hope's new height.

Letting go, yet holding tight,
The dance of dark, the glow of bright.
Beneath it all, though memories sway,
Love will guide our hearts each day.

The Art of Letting Go

In gentle whispers, I release,
Memories fade like autumn leaves.
Each tear a step toward the peace,
Embracing loss, my heart believes.

From shadows deep, new light will spring,
The weight of what was starts to lift.
In every ending, songs we sing,
Turn heavy grief into a gift.

With every breath, I find the space,
To welcome change, to grow anew.
The heart's pure art, a soft embrace,
Of what remains and what's untrue.

I gather strength from what is past,
The burdens start to feel less sore.
Through tangled roots, a future cast,
I learn the art of letting go.

In stillness found, the soul can soar,
Break free from chains, reclaim the sky.
In quiet moments, I explore,
The beauty in goodbye's soft sigh.

Chasing Sunsets Beyond the Dawn

Each daybreak paints a world anew,
Golden tones against the blue.
With every step, my spirit races,
Towards horizons, bright embraced places.

The sun dips low, a fiery treat,
Casting shadows that dance, then fleet.
Chasing dreams on the canvas vast,
Fleeting moments, glowing and fast.

Footprints linger on sandy shores,
Echoes of laughter, heart's open doors.
In twilight's glow, the night begins,
Warmth of memories beneath my skin.

Stars awaken, guiding light,
Illuminating paths of night.
Chasing sunsets, we find our way,
In colors that lead us, come what may.

With every sunset, hope reborn,
A promise wrapped in dusk's soft horn.
In the chase, we learn to see,
The beauty in what's meant to be.

Remnants of a Forgotten Journey

Dusty roads hold stories old,
Whispers of where my heart once strolled.
Each step a memory, faint yet real,
Fragments of truth, time's warm appeal.

Through tangled woods and silent streams,
I tread where once I dared to dream.
With every shadow, a lesson learned,
The fire within, forever burned.

Lost pages of a weathered book,
Ink of experiences in each nook.
Every twist and turn a thread,
Of paths long traveled, now widespread.

I gather pieces, stitch them tight,
A tapestry of wrong and right.
In remnants found, my heart grows still,
The journey's echo, a sacred thrill.

From ashes rise the soul's embrace,
Reclaim the past, find my own place.
In every sigh, hope's soft refrain,
Remnants whisper, I rise again.

The Silence of Old Wounds

In shadows cast by bitter pain,
Where echoes linger, hearts remain.
The silence speaks in haunted halls,
Of love once bright, now but a pall.

Unspoken words like ghosts reside,
In corners where my tears have cried.
Each memory a weight to bear,
Yet in the stillness, I find prayer.

Time's soft touch begins to mend,
The fractured pieces it can tend.
With every silence, strength will grow,
A gentle hand on wounds below.

The heart knows well the scars it wears,
Each mark a chapter, each breath shares.
In quietude, I learn to see,
The beauty that comes from pain's decree.

Embracing whispers of the night,
I find my way, restore the light.
In silent vows, the past can bloom,
The healing power in every room.

The Light Beyond Shadows

In the depth where silence dwells,
A flicker shines, a tale it tells.
Hope ignites like stars in night,
Guiding souls towards the light.

Through valleys dark, we wander free,
With whispers soft, our spirits see.
The dawn will break, the shadows flee,
In every heart, a spark of glee.

We rise from ashes, hearts aflame,
Forging paths, we play the game.
With every step, our fears we tame,
Embracing life, we stake our claim.

From dusk till dawn, we chase the dream,
With every challenge, learn and scheme.
In unity, our hopes will stream,
Together strong, we form a team.

The light beyond, forever near,
In every moment, banishing fear.
With open hearts and minds so clear,
We find our way, the path sincere.

Lasting Impressions of Growth

Roots deepen where the heart resides,
In gentle soil, the spirit hides.
With every storm, we sway and bend,
Resilience blooms, we will transcend.

Time carves lines upon our face,
Each wrinkle tells of life's embrace.
In moments fleeting, wisdom shared,
The beauty found in being prepared.

With laughter's echo, and tears that flow,
We learn to cherish, let our hearts grow.
In gardens rich with joy and pain,
The seeds of love will still remain.

Through trials faced, our courage shines,
In every struggle, growth aligns.
We cultivate our dreams anew,
In fertile ground, our visions brew.

As seasons change, we stand as one,
With open hearts, the journey's fun.
Lasting impressions, how we've soared,
Together bound, we are restored.

Constellations of Future Dreams

In the velvet sky, our wishes gleam,
Fabric woven with every dream.
Stars align in a cosmic dance,
Pointing hearts toward a second chance.

With every heartbeat, visions grow,
In the tapestry of life, we sew.
The constellations whisper clear,
Embrace the path, let go of fear.

From the ashes of yesterday's plight,
We rise anew, seeking the light.
With every heartbeat, dreams will soar,
On wings of hope, forevermore.

Galaxies churn with every thought,
In the universe, we find what's sought.
With eyes wide open, hearts in tune,
We navigate by the light of the moon.

As we journey through this vast expanse,
Finding purpose in every chance.
Constellations of future dreams,
A voyage woven, so it seems.

Embracing the Unknown

In shadows deep, new paths unfold,
Mysteries bloom, waiting to be told.
Hearts leap forth, where fears reside,
Steps unwrap dreams, on the wild side.

A canvas blank, with colors bright,
Every choice leads to a different height.
With every twist, the soul will grow,
In the dance of fate, we learn to flow.

Whispers call from the depths of night,
Guiding stars, our hopes ignite.
Though doubt may grasp, we hold it tight,
For in the dark, there blooms the light.

Paths diverge as time moves on,
Yet daring spirits usher dawn.
In the unknown, we find our song,
Through every trial, we all belong.

Embrace the chaos, cherish the chance,
Life's wild journey is a sacred dance.
With open hearts, let wonders be,
In the arms of fate, we will be free.

Untangling Lives

Threads of fate woven so tight,
In the tapestry, seeking the light.
Lives intersect, paths entwined,
In the chaos, solace we find.

Moments shared, whispers low,
In tangled ties, love does grow.
Journeys crossed on winding roads,
With every burden, the heart explodes.

Memories cling like morning dew,
Soft reflections of me and you.
Each heart's story, a world apart,
Yet still they echo, soul to heart.

Through trials faced and laughter blared,
Bonds emerge, beautifully paired.
In every scar, a lesson learned,
As lives untangle, passion burned.

Together we rise, as fates align,
In unity's grip, forever shine.
In the dance of life, we find our way,
Untangling dreams, day by day.

Footprints in Solitude

Upon the shore, footprints stray,
In solitude's grip, they'll fade away.
Whispers of waves, calling me near,
In silent thoughts, I confront my fear.

Every step marks a fleeting trace,
In the quiet, I find my place.
Beneath the stars, the night unfolds,
In solitude, my heart beholds.

Moments languish, time stands still,
In quietude, I feel the thrill.
Reflections dance on the ocean's face,
Each breath a gift, a soft embrace.

Footsteps lead where shadows play,
In solitude's heart, I drift away.
The world may hush, but echoes stay,
In the silence, a soul's ballet.

To walk alone is to learn and see,
In every heartbeat, I am free.
With footprints left in soft sand's turn,
In solitude's glow, I gladly learn.

Whispers of the Departed

In twilight's veil, they softly call,
Echoes linger, through shadows crawl.
Voices faint on the evening air,
Whispers of love, timeless and rare.

Memory dances on the edge of night,
Guiding souls in ethereal flight.
In gentle breezes, their laughter sways,
Carrying warmth through bygone days.

Stars remind us of tales once spun,
In the silence lingers all that's done.
Though we may part with a heavy heart,
Their essence lives, never to depart.

We see their smiles in the softest light,
In dreams, they wander, day and night.
As shadows fade, love will not cease,
For in our hearts, they find their peace.

So we embrace the night's sweet gift,
The whispers linger, spirits lift.
In every tear, a memory's glow,
The departed stay, through love we know.

Crossing Over

A bridge of dreams we tread with care,
The whispers of the night in the air.
Stars above guide our wandering hearts,
In the distance, a new journey starts.

With every step, the shadows fade,
And daylight breaks, our fears invade.
Yet hope shines bright in every eye,
As we venture forth, the world awry.

Through valleys deep and mountains high,
We chase the clouds that drift and fly.
Hand in hand, we'll face the unknown,
On this path where courage is grown.

Behind us lies what we once knew,
A tapestry of memory's hue.
But forward calls, with promise clear,
In the heart, we hold no fear.

Crossing now, the threshold bends,
A saga new that never ends.
Together we brave the endless sea,
In the journey, forever free.

Letting Nature's Tide Wash Away

The ocean whispers secrets low,
With gentle waves that ebb and flow.
Each grain of sand feels like a sigh,
As moments pass like clouds on high.

Letting go of burdens held,
In nature's arms, our hearts compelled.
The salty breeze, a sweet embrace,
In every wave, we find our place.

With open hands and open heart,
We release the past, a brand new start.
The tide comes in, and out it goes,
In this rhythm, freedom grows.

Green leaves dance in the soft, warm light,
Under the stars that pierce the night.
We breathe in deep, the earth's pure grace,
In nature's tide, we find our space.

So let the waves reshape our souls,
In harmony, we seek our roles.
For in the dance of earth and sea,
We learn to let our spirits be.

The Reluctant Goodbye

With heavy hearts, we stand apart,
Words unspoken weigh on the heart.
A touch, a glance, memories collide,
In the silence, love cannot hide.

One last embrace before we part,
A bittersweet ache within the heart.
The clock ticks on, the moments flee,
Yet in the pain, we feel so free.

Promises linger like morning mist,
In the farewell, a fleeting kiss.
But life moves on with its timeless flow,
In every ending, new beginnings grow.

So take my hand as shadows fall,
This chapter closes, but we stand tall.
Though paths may diverge in endless skies,
The bond remains, love never dies.

In memory's light, you'll ever shine,
A thread of fate forever entwined.
In every tear, a story stays,
In the heart, you'll always blaze.

Eclipsing Old Sunsets

The sun dips low, a fiery ball,
As shadows stretch and evening calls.
Colors bleed into the dusky sky,
In the quiet, the world breathes a sigh.

We gather 'round where memories lay,
In the golden hue of yesterday.
But as the night begins to creep,
New dawns awaken from their sleep.

Letting go of what once was bright,
We turn towards the coming night.
In cosmic dance, the stars ignite,
A reminder of hope's enduring light.

Though sunsets fade, they're not the end,
In every twilight, new paths blend.
For in the dark, we find our way,
Towards dreams that shimmer and sway.

So let the old give way to new,
Embrace the night, let it renew.
For in the eclipse, we see the whole,
An endless journey for the soul.

The Last Page Turned

In shadowed corners, tales unfold,
Memories linger, stories told.
A final chapter, ink runs dry,
Whispers of time, a soft goodbye.

The binding breaks, the heart can sigh,
Each word a tear, each thought a tie.
Yet as I close this weary tome,
I find in endings, I still find home.

The dust may settle, but dreams remain,
In every loss, a lesson gained.
The pages worn, the spine a bend,
A story lives, it never ends.

Waking Up to Tomorrow

The sun peeks through the curtain seams,
A brand-new day, the echo of dreams.
With every breath, the world feels new,
In softest light, my spirit grew.

Birds take flight, their songs arise,
A chorus sweet beneath the skies.
I shake off shadows of yesterday's care,
To embrace the dawn, with hope laid bare.

Each moment whispers, 'You are here,'
In laughter's warmth, in love's bright cheer.
The promise of what tomorrow brings,
Awakens joy in simple things.

Letting Go of Ghosts

In haunted halls where silence dwells,
Old echoes linger, the heart repels.
Each whisper lost, a tale undone,
The past retreats, a fading sun.

Hands once held now slip from grasp,
Time's cruel flow, we can't outlast.
Yet in the light of morning's glow,
I learn the art of letting go.

The weight of burdens starts to lift,
In every ending, a subtle gift.
The ghosts may fade, but lessons stay,
They teach us how to find our way.

A New Dawn Rising

From depths of night, the light breaks free,
A canvas fresh, as far as we see.
With every heartbeat, life ignites,
In vibrant hues, the future excites.

Mountains climb, the valleys call,
With courage strong, we rise and fall.
Each dawn a chance to paint anew,
To step with faith in skies of blue.

The stars may dim, yet dreams still glint,
In every breath, there's hope to hint.
A symphony of life, we compose,
With every sunrise, our spirit grows.

Moments That No Longer Define

Shadows whisper secrets, soft and low,
Fleeting memories dance, where time won't go.
Fragments of laughter lost in the breeze,
Echoes of dreams fade, like autumn leaves.

Chasing horizons, we wander away,
What once felt tethered, now drifts astray.
The heart finds solace in stories untold,
Moments like petals, in silence unfold.

Reflections in puddles, the past starts to glow,
Yet, the future blooms in the seeds we sow.
Chains of the past can't bind us for long,
We rise from the ashes, brave and strong.

Each heartbeat a stitch in the fabric of now,
We wave goodbye to what we won't allow.
Forging new pathways, let go of the blind,
In every new dawn, our peace we will find.

Learning to cherish the lessons we've learned,
Through fires of sorrow, our spirits have burned.
Moving onward, we tread lightly, unconfined,
Embracing the moments that no longer bind.

The Veil of Yesterday's Grief

In shadows cloaked, where silence does creep,
The weight of sorrow, in whispers, we keep.
A tapestry woven with threads of despair,
The veil of yesterday hangs heavy in air.

Each tear a testament, each sigh a song,
The heart learns to carry what feels so wrong.
Yet in the darkness, a flicker stays bright,
Hope emerges softly, like stars in the night.

Layers of longing entwine with the dawn,
We rise through the ashes, reborn and drawn.
The echoes of pain, like ghosts, start to fade,
In the light of acceptance, new paths are laid.

With every heartbeat, a new start arrives,
In grief's gentle arms, our spirit survives.
The veil may be heavy, but strength it can lend,
To navigate through, where healing transcends.

We learn to remember but choose not to dwell,
In the garden of memories, where love still swells.
Each day a reminder, we stand and believe,
That the veil of yesterday can help us conceive.

A Symphony of Unwritten Chapters

Pages unturned, a book yet to write,
Dreams linger softly, igniting the night.
Notes of a symphony, sweet melodies hum,
In the heart's quiet corners, new stories come.

Ink on the fingers, adventures await,
The canvas unmarked, inviting our fate.
With each whispered wish, a new seed we sow,
A journey unfolding, with wonders to show.

Casting our visions on star-speckled skies,
We leap into realms where possibility lies.
Forth from the shadows, we courageously leap,
In the orchestra's chorus, our promises keep.

The rhythm of life, a dance of delight,
A tapestry woven in gold and in light.
The notes blend together, crafting our song,
In this symphony's heart, we finally belong.

Each chapter unwritten, a chance to explore,
To find the true essence of all we adore.
In the quietest moments, our spirits engage,
Creating a melody that fills every page.

Crossroads in the Twilight

At dusk's gentle edge, where paths intertwine,
Footsteps echo softly, hearts start to align.
Two roads diverge under indigo skies,
A choice on the horizon, where possibility lies.

Whispers of fate guide the wandering soul,
In the stillness of twilight, we seek to be whole.
Navigating shadows, the doubts start to wane,
The pulse of the future beats strong in our veins.

Each crossroad a mirror reflecting our truth,
The fears and the hopes of our vibrant youth.
With courage ignited, we step into fate,
Embracing the unknown, no longer we wait.

Veils of uncertainty shimmer in gold,
Lessons learned deeply, with stories retold.
As stars start to flicker, decisions take flight,
In the dance of the evening, we've found our light.

With every deep breath, commitment is made,
To travel the roads, let adventure cascade.
These crossroads in twilight beckon us near,
To weave our own future, to conquer our fear.

Shadows of Yesterday's Echoes

In the dusk where whispers weave,
Shadows rise, hearts believe.
Flickers of laughter, now adrift,
Echoes linger, dreams they gift.

Ghostly forms in twilight's grasp,
Fading time, we reach and clasp.
Memories dance like autumn leaves,
In their flight, the heart deceives.

Through the haze, a soft lament,
Fragments of joy forever spent.
In silence, we hear the past's call,
In shadows, we rise and fall.

Every heartbeat, a tethered sigh,
Moments captured, yet they fly.
In the echoes, we find our way,
Shadows linger, night turns to day.

Time moves on, yet here we stand,
In yesterday's embrace, hand in hand.
Through the shadows, we will roam,
In every echo, we find home.

Unraveled Threads of Memory

A tapestry of time laid bare,
Threads of laughter, threads of care.
Each strand a story, softly spun,
In the fabric, we come undone.

Fingers trace the worn-out seams,
Hearing whispers of forgotten dreams.
Hopes entangled, love's sweet thrill,
In woven tales, the heart is still.

Colors fade like twilight skies,
Yet the truth in silence lies.
Unraveled threads, yet strong they weave,
In our minds, they never leave.

Moments linger, a bittersweet taste,
In recalling, we find no waste.
Softly, gently, the memories flow,
In every heartbeat, they gently grow.

As seasons change, the threads may fray,
But in the weave, we find our way.
With every stitch, a life we trace,
Unraveled threads in time and space.

The Weight of What Once Was

Beneath the weight of whispered dreams,
Lies a past woven in moonbeams.
Carried softly, the burden's deep,
In shadows linger, memories keep.

Time has draped a heavy veil,
In the silence, the echoes wail.
Every sigh, a whispered pain,
In the heart, a soft refrain.

Moments linger like morning dew,
Reflecting all we've said and knew.
Yet through the weight, we stand so tall,
With every tear, we rise, we fall.

In the quiet, the thoughts collide,
What once was, now cannot hide.
We gather strength from loss endured,
In this weight, we find the pure.

For every shadow holds a light,
In the past, we find our fight.
The weight we carry, now our guide,
Through every storm, we do abide.

Fading Footprints on the Shore

Footprints lie in golden sand,
Traces left by love's own hand.
Waves roll in to softly erase,
Memories lost in time and space.

With every tide, the past departs,
Leaving echoes in our hearts.
Fading slowly like distant stars,
Guiding us through our silent scars.

Seagulls cry as the sun dips low,
Casting shadows on the flow.
Each step taken, a story told,
In the silence, whispers unfold.

Yet in the depths, a truth remains,
In fleeting joy, there's no more pain.
Footprints fade but love's embraced,
In every heart, the trace is placed.

So as we walk on shifting ground,
In every loss, new hope is found.
Fading footprints, but we explore,
In every wave, we learn to soar.

Silent Goodbyes

In the quiet of dusk, we part,
Words left unspoken weigh heavy on hearts.
A glance shared, a tear in the night,
Silent goodbyes fade out of sight.

Footsteps linger on the worn path,
Ghosts of laughter, shadows of wrath.
Memories dance like leaves in the breeze,
Whispers of love, a soft heart's ease.

Promises made under starlit skies,
But fate has its way, and time swiftly flies.
I hold your essence, like stars in my hand,
Though distance stretches, our bond will withstand.

Each moment cherished, forever we'll stand,
In the echoes of time, in a vibrant land.
Though journeys diverge, in dreams we will meet,
Silent goodbyes won't taste of defeat.

As shadows lengthen, I breathe in your light,
Your spirit remains, a beacon at night.
Farewell for now, but not the end,
In every heartbeat, you still transcend.

The Last Train to Nowhere

Under the moon, a whistle does cry,
The last train departs, leaving hope to fly.
A gentle thud, as wheels kiss the track,
Into the unknown, there's no looking back.

Conversations fade, like smoke in the air,
Empty seats echo with unspoken care.
Stars streak by, a brief, fleeting glance,
On this midnight ride, we dare to dance.

Through shadows and light, a journey unfolds,
With stories entwined, golden threads bold.
Whispers of dreams shatter as we roam,
This train of lost souls is heading for home.

The engine's roar lulls the weary to sleep,
As valleys and mountains, together they sweep.
Through the windows, we catch a soft sigh,
The last train departs, a farewell to why.

And as dawn breaks, we meet the new day,
Where memories linger, the heart finds a way.
Though nowhere awaits, I'll hold you so near,
In the silence of tracks, there's nothing to fear.

Fields of Memory

Amidst the tall grass, our laughter once grew,
Fields of memory painted in every hue.
Sunshine and shadows danced on our skin,
Each moment a treasure, where love did begin.

Butterflies flutter, like dreams in the air,
Whispers of childhood, both tender and rare.
The scent of wildflowers drifts on the breeze,
Echoes of innocence, a soft heart's tease.

Seasons have changed, yet still I can feel,
The warmth of those summers, so vibrant, so real.
In every petal, a story unfolds,
A tapestry woven with glimmers of gold.

Though time marches on, and we're miles apart,
These fields of memory remain in my heart.
With every sunrise, I feel your embrace,
In the rustling leaves, I find your grace.

So I wander these fields, where our dreams ran free,
In shadows and sunlight, you're always with me.
Though life's road may shift, and paths intertwine,
In fields of memory, our souls brightly shine.

Driftwood on Shifting Sands

Along the shore, where the waves kiss the land,
Driftwood lies scattered, untouched by a hand.
Each piece a story, weathered and worn,
Carved by the ocean, in silence reborn.

The tides come and go, a dance ever true,
As grains of sand whisper secrets to the blue.
In the twilight glow, shadows stretch and sway,
Nature's own canvas, painted by day.

Memories wash up, like shells on the beach,
Lessons from tides, life's truths they teach.
The heartbeat of nature, a timeless refrain,
A symphony playing through joy and through pain.

As stars emerge, the horizon ignites,
With promises whispered on warm summer nights.
Each driftwood sentinel stands tall and proud,
Guardians of stories, of dreams that enshroud.

So let the winds blow and the tempests rage,
We're all like driftwood, turning a page.
Finding our place, like ships on the strand,
Together, we weather, through life's shifting sand.

Gossamer Threads of Yesterday

In the dawn's soft embrace we weave,
Memories dance like leaves on a breeze.
Whispers of laughter, shadows of sighs,
Stitching the fabric where time lies.

Threads of gossamer, fragile and light,
Hold tales of longing in morning's light.
Moments suspended in twilight's glow,
Each whisper a secret, the heart's gentle flow.

The tapestry speaks of faces long gone,
Yet echoes their voices in every dawn.
Faded pictures, of moments unspun,
Life weaves a story, never quite done.

Through the veil of the past, we still peer,
Chasing the shadows, we hold dear.
In threads intertwined, we find our way,
Carrying stories that long for the day.

Gossamer threads of yesterday's light,
Guide us through memories, holding us tight.
In each gentle stitch, a world is defined,
An artful reminder of love intertwined.

Shadows That Fade

As twilight drapes the earth in grey,
Shadows stretch and slowly sway.
Fleeting forms on pavement cold,
Tales of the past in whispers told.

Beneath the stars, the night takes hold,
We carve our dreams from stories old.
Yet shadows linger, soft and thin,
Echoes of places where we've been.

Time drips like water from hands of fate,
Shadows that fade never hesitate.
Each moment lost, the heart does ache,
For paths untraveled, those dreams we make.

In the silence, a memory glows,
Remnants of laughter, the heart's warm throes.
Though shadows may fade as we chase the dawn,
Their essence lingers, love's gentle song.

Weaving through life, as shadows blend,
Each fleeting image, a lover, a friend.
Though time may erase what once held weight,
Shadows of love hold stories innate.

When the Heart Moves On

In the soft hush of a fading day,
When silence speaks more than words can say.
The heart learns to wander, to let things be,
Finding solace in what sets it free.

Like a river that flows with unyielding grace,
Love leaves its mark, then steps from the trace.
Though echoes linger in chambers unknown,
When the heart moves on, it finds its own home.

Memories drift like leaves in the air,
Each whisper a promise of love and care.
In the warmth of the sun, in the cool evening breeze,
The heart stitches hope with delicate ease.

Letting go gently, as petals unfold,
Time weaves new stories, embers of gold.
When the heart finds peace and the soul takes flight,
The journey continues, embracing the light.

So here's to the moments that help us grow,
When the heart moves on, it sets the flow.
With grace on its wings, it learns to embrace,
The beauty of living in love's warm space.

Flickering Frames of Time

In flickering frames, the memories play,
Captured in moments, both joyful and grey.
Each shutter click echoes life's sweet refrain,
Reminding us gently of love's sweet pain.

Vivid portraits of laughter and tears,
Woven together through joys and fears.
The heart holds the light as days start to wane,
In flickering frames, feelings remain.

Time dances lightly, a delicate waltz,
Framing our memories, never one false.
Each snapshot a treasure, a piece of our soul,
In every turn of fate, we find ourselves whole.

We wander through scenes both tender and bright,
A tapestry woven with day and night.
Flickering frames tell the stories we seek,
In silence, they speak of the joy and the bleak.

So let us embrace each image we see,
For flickering frames hold what's meant to be.
In the gallery of hearts, every moment shines,
Breathing in love through the passage of time.

Crumpled Letters of Goodbye

In shadows cast by fading light,
Fingers trace the words of night.
Tears fall on paper, love's sweet grace,
Memories linger in this space.

Crumpled letters piled high,
Promises whispered, now a sigh.
Each crease a story left untold,
Hearts wrapped in nostalgia's fold.

The ink has blurred with distant years,
Every line, a mix of fears.
Yet in the crumple lies a spark,
A voice that echoes through the dark.

These tokens of a love once bright,
Cast away in fading light.
In every wrinkle, a shadow seen,
The love we had, the in-between.

And though we part, the letters stay,
A testament of yesterday.
In whispered winds and silent nights,
They carry forth our shared delights.

Windswept Hopes and Future Paths

Upon the hill where flowers sway,
Windswept dreams drift far away.
Each gust a chance, a silent call,
To chase the dreams, to risk it all.

Beneath the sky, so vast and bright,
We gather hopes to set alight.
The whispered winds guide us near,
To paths unknown, casting out fear.

With every step, we shape our fate,
Embracing change, we learn, create.
The future beckons, a canvas wide,
With open hearts, we turn the tide.

In twilight's glow, our shadows blend,
Windswept hopes, forever ascend.
Together we'll forge new trails to roam,
Hand in hand, we find our home.

Through valleys low and mountains steep,
Our dreams take flight, our promises keep.
Windswept hopes will always guide,
As we walk forth, side by side.

Ripples in the River of Time

In water's grace, the ripples flow,
Each moment shared begins to glow.
Time whispers secrets soft and low,
A dance of past, a gentle show.

The river bends with each embrace,
Reminds us of our sacred space.
While clocks may tick and seasons change,
In stillness, we can rearrange.

And as we float on currents wide,
The echoes of our hearts confide.
Ripples trace the love we've worn,
In every twist, our hopes reborn.

Though time may strain and moments part,
Each ripple flows close to the heart.
We savor now, we cherish then,
The river's song will call again.

Through tranquil nights and mornings bright,
We witness ripples dance in light.
In harmony, our stories rhyme,
As we drift forth, in the river of time.

Ascending from Ashes of Memory

In silence deep, old ashes lay,
Fragments of dreams that flew away.
Yet in the dark, a spark ignites,
Whispers of hope in starry nights.

From embers glow, new visions rise,
Beneath the weight of past goodbyes.
Phoenix hearts begin to soar,
Life's symphony calling for more.

We weave our pain into the thread,
A tapestry of tears we shed.
For from the ashes, bold we stand,
Reclaiming dreams with outstretched hands.

Memory's ghosts may try to bind,
But strength within, we will find.
Together we'll ascend the skies,
Defy the fall, embrace the rise.

In every breath, the past retreats,
As future blooms in vibrant beats.
Ascending from the ashes bright,
We find our way, we claim our light.

Heartbeats Beyond Old Walls

In shadows deep, whispers sigh,
Echoes linger, time drifts by.
Old bricks cradle tales of yore,
Heartbeats pulse from every door.

Ghosts of laughter, secrets shared,
Silent moments, hearts laid bare.
Rustling leaves and creaking beams,
Weaving stories from our dreams.

Beneath the moon, the silence sings,
Reviving hope, eternal springs.
A tapestry of love and loss,
In every crack, the weight, the gloss.

Yearning souls, we seek the light,
Finding warmth in the cold night.
With every heartbeat, walls will sway,
Bringing forth a brand new day.

Old walls hold what we can't see,
A dance of lives, wild and free.
In every heartbeat, tales reside,
Beyond old walls, our hearts confide.

The Language of Forgotten Places

In twilight's glow, whispers fade,
Ancient paths where shadows wade.
Rusty signs and crumbled stone,
The language speaks, though we're alone.

Beneath the dust, the echoes hum,
A symphony of times long gone.
Mystic tales on swirling air,
In every twist, the past laid bare.

We walk where silence softly calls,
In hidden corners, memory sprawls.
Unraveled threads of faded dreams,
Amongst the ruins, hope still gleams.

Each lingering scent, a story told,
Of distant hearts and lives of old.
We listen close, as spirits rise,
The language sings beneath the skies.

In these forgotten, sacred spaces,
Time stands still, love's warm embraces.
Together we find what once was lost,
In the language of places, we pay the cost.

Dreams That Cross the Threshold

In quiet nights, our visions soar,
Past the line of nevermore.
Whispers beckon, softly glow,
Dreams awaken, hearts in tow.

Underneath the starlit sky,
We seek answers, let them fly.
Crossing borders of our mind,
In dreams, new worlds we find.

Each threshold crossed, a moment bare,
A reflection held in midnight air.
Fragments, colors, dance and blend,
To realities that never end.

We share our hopes, our fears align,
In liminal spaces, souls entwine.
At dawn's embrace, we chase the light,
Carrying dreams into the fight.

For every dream that graces night,
Is a beacon, a guiding light.
Together we rise, together we quest,
In dreams that cross, we find our rest.

New Roots in Untamed Soil

In vibrant fields, we stake our claim,
New roots stretch wide, wild and untamed.
With every shelter, hope takes flight,
Planting seeds, we spark the light.

Through seasons harsh, our spirits bloom,
Breaking ground, dispelling gloom.
Tenacious hearts in harmony,
In untamed soil, we're wild and free.

With every raindrop, life unfolds,
Stories whispered, earth retold.
Connecting hearts beneath the sun,
In unity, our roots have won.

From trembling hands, a harvest grows,
In every struggle, love bestows.
Together we brave the storms of fate,
Nurturing dreams that never wait.

In this wild embrace, we find our place,
New branches twist in a warm embrace.
As roots entwine, we paint our tale,
In untamed soil, we shall prevail.

Circles of Time that Fade Away

In the quiet of the night,
Whispers dance with stars so bright,
Moments slip like grains of sand,
In our dreams, we take a stand.

Memories wane, but hearts remain,
Holding on through joy and pain,
Time, a thief, but also friend,
In its arms, we blend and mend.

Shadows stretch and colors blend,
As we search for timeless ends,
Circular paths that lead us back,
Through the light and into black.

Eyes that gaze through fading days,
Find the light in whispered ways,
As the sun sets, we understand,
Time, like art, slips through our hands.

Yet we walk this fragile line,
With each heartbeat, we entwine,
Creating circles, bright and gray,
Circles of time that fade away.

The Echo of Doors Left Ajar

Faintest sounds in quiet halls,
Footsteps linger, then they fall,
Echoes whisper tales untold,
Of hidden rooms and hearts so bold.

A door stands open, just a crack,
Inviting light and shadows back,
What lies beyond the threshold's seam?
A world of hope, a fleeting dream.

Secrets dwell in what was past,
In whispers shared, in shadows cast,
Every echo sings the song,
Of places where we still belong.

With every breath, the silence sighs,
As moments pass like fleeting flies,
We chase the sound that lingers near,
In the echo, memories clear.

So we stand with hearts exposed,
In the glow where love has flowed,
Through the frames, our dreams have sparred,
In the echo of doors left ajar.

Journeying Beyond the Familiar

Footprints trace the soil of dreams,
Where the river twists and gleams,
Each turn holds a brand new face,
In the wild, we find our place.

Mountains rise, the sky expands,
In the mist, we make our plans,
With every step, we leave behind,
The tethered thoughts that cloud the mind.

Beyond the fields of known and safe,
We chase the winds, our hearts brave,
Each horizon opens wide,
In the journey, fears subside.

Underneath the starlit skies,
We discover unseen ties,
The paths we walk, though strange and new,
Bring us closer, me to you.

So take my hand, let's roam and soar,
To places where we've not been before,
Journeying forth, our spirits will rise,
Beyond the familiar, to endless skies.

Harvesting Stars from Old Skies

Crimson twilight paints the land,
As nightfall wraps with gentle hand,
We look above, where wishes glow,
To harvest stars from skies we know.

Each shimmering light, a tale to tell,
Of hearts once lost, of loves that fell,
In the darkness, we seek and dive,
Harvesting dreams that still survive.

With every glint, we weave the past,
Threads of futures, shadows cast,
In the open night, let thoughts collide,
Stars remind us, time will bide.

With gentle hands and hopeful eyes,
We gather glittering, vast goodbyes,
Each star, a promise, a memory shared,
In the heavens, we find we're spared.

So lift your gaze, the night is wide,
With every star, let joy abide,
We'll find our peace, and in the gray,
Keep harvesting stars from old skies.

In the Wake of Yesterday

Memories linger like shadows cast,
Whispers of laughter, echoes of the past.
Footprints on beaches, fading away,
Carried by tides, beneath the gray.

Promises broken, like glass on the floor,
Shattered reflections, lost evermore.
Yet hope still glimmers, a faint distant star,
Guiding the heart, no matter how far.

In the wake of yesterday, we rise anew,
Finding our strength, in skies ever blue.
Each dawn a canvas, unmarked, unclaimed,
With colors of courage, unashamed.

Though storms may linger, and clouds may fall,
Resilience beckons, through it all.
We'll write our stories, with pen in hand,
In the wake of yesterday, together we'll stand.

Every ending births a brand new start,
Leaving behind what's torn apart.
With every heartbeat, a chance to believe,
In the wake of yesterday, we learn to receive.

Carving Paths in New Soil

With every step, the earth beneath,
We carve our paths, with grit and belief.
New soil awaits, rich and untamed,\nPlanting our dreams,
forever unclaimed.

The sun on our backs, the breeze in our hair,
We push through the doubts, embrace what is rare.
Tilling the land with hopes intertwined,
In the dance of the future, our hearts aligned.

Yet roots of the past may cling to the ground,
Whispers of what was, in silence profound.
But we are the farmers, sowing with care,
In fields of tomorrow, a sacred affair.

Through trials and laughter, we learn to grow,
Watered by wisdom, in rivers that flow.
The paths that we carve, both bold and anew,
In this garden of life, we find our true hue.

Carving our journeys, with dreams as our wheel,
In new soil we flourish, embracing what's real.
Together we'll wander, hand in hand, side by side,
For in carving our paths, our spirits abide.

Burning Bridges Behind

Fires ignite where paths once crossed,
Ashes of memories, bitterly tossed.
The heat of the moment can scorch and consume,
Yet from the embers, new blossoms can bloom.

Choices made echo, in silence they lay,
Perceptions once cherished, now fade away.
The crackle of wood, a final goodbye,
As we stand on the edge, with hearts open wide.

Each flame a lesson, a truth to embrace,
The shadows of doubt now fading in space.
For bridges once sturdy, may weigh us down,
Setting things ablaze, we loosen the crown.

With courage ignited, we soar from the ground,
Leaving behind what no longer surrounds.
The skies may darken, the winds may moan,
But in burning bridges, we claim our own throne.

In the distance, new horizons emerge,
With flames that once bound us, now we converge.
Burning the past, we rise from the ash,
In the glow of tomorrow, we take our bold flash.

The Heart's Quiet Exodus

In the still of the night, a whisper takes flight,
The heart seeks solace, wrapped in moonlight.
Silent goodbyes, as shadows retreat,
In the softest of echoes, the soul feels complete.

A journey unfolding, not marked by a map,
The compass within charts a gentle gap.
Each step a release, a sigh of relief,
In the heart's quiet exodus, we find our belief.

Through valleys of silence and mountains of peace,
The burdens we carry begin to release.
In tender embraces, we learn to let go,
With every soft heartbeat, new courage will grow.

Though paths may be winding, and darkness may creep,
In the heart's quiet exodus, we learn to leap.
Trusting the journey, as we merge with the light,
Finding our way in the warmth of the night.

With every departure, a promise anew,
The heart's quiet exodus, a dreaming view.
As we wander and drift, wherever we roam,
In the quiet of hearts, we create our true home.

Tides of Change

Waves crash upon the shore,
Whispers of what was before.
In the ebb, we learn to grow,
As the currents start to flow.

Every tide brings forth new dreams,
Caught in life's ever-shifting seams.
With each rise, hope's light remains,
Guiding hearts through joy and pains.

Beneath the moon's watchful eye,
We find the strength to say goodbye.
In the silence, secrets leak,
In the turning tide, we seek.

Change is fierce, yet gentle, too,
Like the dawn, fresh with morning dew.
Step by step, we walk the lines,
Embracing fate, the heart inclines.

The ocean's breath, a song we hear,
Filling our souls with needed cheer.
Through rising tides, we learn to dance,
In this rhythm, we find our chance.

The Fading Imprint

Footprints captured in the sand,
Whispers of where we used to stand.
As the tide takes them away,
Memories fade with the day.

Time like water slips through hands,
Echoes linger, yet it expands.
Moments cherished, lost in flow,
What remains we hardly know.

In the dusk, reflections glide,
Silent wishes, dreams reside.
What was vibrant slowly dims,
Yet in shadows, hope still swims.

A light that flickers in the night,
Guiding us with its gentle sight.
Fading paths and whispered lanes,
Yet in the heart, love still reigns.

Though the imprints fade away,
In our hearts, they softly stay.
While the waves erase the signs,
The essence of joy still shines.

Nightfall on Old Paths

Under the cloak of twilight's grace,
Familiar roads we softly trace.
Memories linger in the breeze,
Whispers shared beneath the trees.

The sun dips low, stars ignite,
Guiding us through the coming night.
Echoes of laughter fill the air,
Reminders of love, forever there.

Old paths creak with every step,
Stories held that we've all kept.
In the shadows, truths unfold,
Lessons learned and tales retold.

Nightfall wraps the world in peace,
As the noise of life will cease.
Beneath the moon, our spirits soar,
In the quiet, we find our core.

As dreams intermingle with the stars,
We see past life's little scars.
On these paths, we find our way,
Guided by love's light each day.

Seeds of Future Growth

In the soil, we bury dreams,
Nurtured by sunlight's golden beams.
Hope takes root, strong and bold,
In the hush, new stories unfold.

Watered by tears and laughter,
Each moment a chapter after.
As seasons shift, we find our place,
In this dance, we seek embrace.

The garden whispers tales of yore,
Of journeys taken, and so much more.
With patience, blooms begin to rise,
Coloring the world, a sweet surprise.

Life's lessons sprout from every side,
In the chaos, peace will abide.
From tiny seeds, great stories grow,
In unity, love starts to show.

As we nurture what we've sown,
A fragrant future we can own.
In every blossom, hope is found,
In life's embrace, we are all bound.

In Search of New Beginnings

Each dawn whispers softly, we rise anew,
With hopes like petals, kissed by dew.
The past behind us, we cast away,
Embracing the light of another day.

Paths untrodden lie before our feet,
With every step, the rhythm's sweet.
New chapters waiting to be spun,
In the tapestry of life, we've just begun.

The heart beats louder, yearning to feel,
As we navigate the vast, the real.
In the garden of dreams, we dare to tread,
Watering seeds of what lies ahead.

With courage as our faithful guide,
We leap into the vast, the wide.
In search of moments yet to unfold,
Finding treasures richer than gold.

So here's to the journey, brave and bold,
With stories of love and laughter told.
In search of beginnings, we take our flight,
Chasing the warm embrace of light.

Breathing Life into the Unknown

In shadows deep where whispers dwell,
We stand on edges, hearts that swell.
The unknown beckons with a siren's call,
Promising wonders beyond the fall.

Each breath we take ignites the brave,
With every heartbeat, we learn to crave.
The stories waiting in untold lands,
Are written by those who dare to stand.

Hands open wide, we catch the dreams,
Floating like clouds on silver beams.
In the depths of fear, we find our fire,
Constructing courage from pure desire.

With every whisper of a new dawn,
We gather strength, from dusk till dawn.
Breathing life into the paths unknown,
A canvas painted with seeds we've sown.

So let the winds guide our wayward flight,
To horizons aglow with promise bright.
As we journey forth to what lies ahead,
Creating tales where none have tread.

The Canvas of Untouched Dreams

In twilight's glow, we halt and gaze,
At the canvas stretched through the misty haze.
With brushes dipped in hopes and fears,
We paint our dreams, through laughter and tears.

Each stroke whispers secrets once held tight,
In colors that dance, vivid and bright.
Untouched landscapes call to our soul,
A melody rising, making us whole.

The palette mixes both light and dark,
In the silence, we hear creation's spark.
Forming visions that shimmer and sway,
In the realm of dreams, we long to play.

Threads of twilight weave into night,
As our spirits take flight in pure delight.
With every brushstroke, tales intertwine,
A world reborn, forever divine.

So here we linger, at the edge of time,
Crafting our stories, pure and sublime.
On the canvas of dreams yet to be,
We find our freedom, our destiny.

Frosted Windows of Yesterday

Through frosted windows, the past appears,
Veiled in whispers of forgotten years.
Each flake of frost holds stories untold,
Of dreams once vibrant, now faded and cold.

With every breath, we fog up the glass,
Revealing the moments, the memories pass.
A glimpse of laughter, a shadow of pain,
In the tapestry woven, we search for the gain.

Behind each pane, the echoes remain,
Of love shared, of loss, of gain.
Yet through the chill, the warmth is found,
In the essence of what still surrounds.

We trace our fingers on icy panes,
Mapping the joy, the struggles, the chains.
Through frostbitten dreams, we yearn to thaw,
Unlocking the lessons, embracing the raw.

With windows aglow in the vibrant light,
We step into mornings, shedding the night.
Through frosted windows, we view afar,
The beauty in yesterday, our guiding star.

Tracing the Line of Time

Moments slip like grains of sand,
Worn edges fade from the hand.
Memories cling like autumn leaves,
Dancing softly, like whispered eves.

Time weaves tales in silent sighs,
With every heartbeat, a new arise.
The past is painted in twilight hues,
While dreams emerge in morning's dew.

Each tick resounds in endless space,
A fleeting shadow, a lingering trace.
In every echo, a story unfolds,
Chasing the warmth of days of gold.

We pause and ponder, the years that fleet,
Dancing shadows under time's discreet.
With open hearts and minds that dream,
We soar beyond the silent stream.

Each moment cherished, forever held,
In the tapestry of life, we meld.
Tracing the lines of what will come,
In the quiet hum, we find our drum.

Beyond the Echoing Walls

Within the chambers, silence reigns,
Ghosts of laughter fill the grains.
Footsteps echo on weathered stone,
Whispers linger where love had grown.

Faded laughter and soft embraces,
Time erodes these sacred places.
Windows watch the world outside,
As memories swell, as if to hide.

In corners dark, where shadows blend,
Fragile moments never end.
Haunted dreams in every hall,
Reverberate with softest call.

Each door ajar, a world unknown,
In every crack, a story sewn.
Secrets dance in the twilight glow,
Revealing truths we yearn to know.

Beyond these walls, the heart takes flight,
In silent hopes, we seek the light.
The echo fades, yet love remains,
In every heartbeat, joy retains.

Sifting Through the Ashes

In the embers where dreams have flown,
Whispers linger, softly grown.
Scattered remnants, tales untold,
A dance of shadows, a glint of gold.

The past still breathes in every spark,
Flickering bright against the dark.
Fragments of joy, echoes of pain,
A phoenix rises from every stain.

Through the ashes, we sift and comb,
Finding beauty in what was home.
Old scars shimmer, bathed in light,
Reclaiming warmth from the quiet night.

Time has tempered the flames we knew,
In every heartbeat, a chance to renew.
What once was lost, we hold so dear,
For in the ash, new dreams appear.

Sifting gently, we find our way,
From sorrow's grip to a bright new day.
Each shard of memory softly calls,
In the silence, the heart enthralls.

Transformation at Twilight

As daylight dims and shadows play,
A world unfurls at close of day.
Colors mingle in a whispered blush,
Nature dances in twilight's hush.

The sky ignites in shades of fire,
Transforming dreams into desire.
Each star awakens, a breath in flight,
Filling the void with soft starlight.

In the cool embrace of evening's grace,
Fears dissolve in the velvet space.
Hope emerges on the horizon line,
In every heartbeat, the stars align.

Change sweeps in on wings of night,
For every end, a new delight.
Within the stillness, we find our way,
Embracing the magic of night and day.

Transformation blooms in the dusk's embrace,
Rebirth blossoms, a tender trace.
At twilight's edge, we learn to be,
In every moment, infinite possibility.

Farewell to Familiar Faces

In shadows cast by parting light,
We bid adieu to days so bright.
With laughter fading into air,
Memories linger, yet none compare.

The street we walked now feels so wide,
Echoes of voices that once confide.
Each corner holds a whispered tale,
As we set sail on winds that wail.

Faces turn like autumn leaves,
Carried by time, the heart believes.
Yet pain entwines with every smile,
For distance stretches every mile.

In photograph and fleeting glance,
A tapestry woven in chance.
Though paths diverge and dreams align,
We'll hold the moments, yours and mine.

With every step, we forge ahead,
Yet in our hearts, the words unsaid.
Farewell, dear friends, till we meet near,
In dreams, we soar, we find you here.

Archways to Unseen Realms

Beneath the sky, where shadows blend,
Archways lead to worlds unpened.
A step beyond the twilight haze,
In whispered winds, life's dance amaze.

Cobblestones of ages past,
Guide the way through times amassed.
With every arch, a story swells,
In echoes deep where mystery dwells.

Through veils of mist, the light shimmers,
The heart listens as fate glimmers.
With courage gathered, we explore,
Each portal inspires us to soar.

Beyond the realm of what we see,
Lies magic waiting to be free.
So take my hand, let's step anew,
For every dream leads close to true.

With hearts entwined in fate's embrace,
The journey calls, we'll find our place.
Through archways framed by starlit skies,
Together, love, we'll reach the prize.

The Unwritten Journey

Each dawn unveils a page unturned,
With ink yet fresh, the spirit yearned.
In silence whispers, fate draws near,
Charting pathways through joy and fear.

With footsteps light, we wander through,
A dance of dreams in skies so blue.
Each moment calls, a voice sincere,
Guiding us onward, year by year.

Stories build as dew meets grass,
In sacred time, our ages pass.
Each heartbeat echoes tales untold,
In colors bright, bold and gold.

The road unwinds like threads of fate,
In laughter shared, we elevate.
While horizons beckon with their light,
Together, love, we'll take to flight.

Though chapters close and pages turn,
In every twist, there's much to learn.
The journey's spark ignites our way,
In every dawn, a brand new day.

Thorns of Old Resentments

In tangled briars lie hidden scars,
The shadows cast by bitter wars.
With every thorn, a story bleeds,
Of broken trust and faded deeds.

Yet time, it seems, can mend the fray,
As petals bloom where pain held sway.
With gentle hands, we soothe the ache,
Turning hate to love's sweet wake.

We gather thorns, embrace the strife,
To shape a path, a clearer life.
Through heavy hearts and troubled nights,
Hope flickers soft, igniting lights.

In gardens rich with lessons learned,
From thorny pasts, resilience earned.
We find the strength to let love grow,
And with each breath, the heart beats slow.

The scars may linger, yet we rise,
In forgiving light, we realize.
That through the thorns, we've found our song,
With love to guide us, we belong.

So come, let's weave our broken seams,
In unity, we'll chase our dreams.
Embracing both the joy and tears,
Together, love, we conquer fears.

Pastels of the Past

Faded hues of yesteryears,
Whisper softly through my mind.
Memories in gentle peers,
In pastel strokes, they've intertwined.

Lost laughter in the afternoon,
Resting beneath the cherry tree.
A simple, sweet, nostalgic tune,
Plays softly, just for you and me.

The sun dips low, a golden sigh,
While shadows stretch and dance,
With colors that will never die,
They linger still in sweet romance.

Each moment blooms, a petaled grace,
Time's canvas, rich and warm.
With every smile, I see your face,
In pastels, our love takes form.

So let us dip in memory's ink,
And paint again those days gone by.
Within each shade, I start to think,
That love remains, though time may fly.

The Dance of the Unbound

In twilight's mist, they start to rise,
A ballet of the wild and free.
No strings to hold, no tethered ties,
They twirl like leaves upon the sea.

With laughter bright, and spirits bold,
Each movement speaks of dreams embraced.
They twine with stars, in silver gold,
A waltz with time, a breathless chase.

Their feet caress the moonlit ground,
Embracing whispers of the night.
In shadowed worlds, where joy is found,
They dance with all their hearts alight.

Through forests deep and mountains high,
They follow rhythms pure and true.
In the vast expanse of the sky,
The dance of the unbound is you.

So let your spirit take its flight,
Through realms where dreams and wishes meet.
In endless joy, through day and night,
For boundless love makes life complete.

Voices from Afar

Echoes linger in the breeze,
Carrying tales of ancient lore.
Whispers float through swaying trees,
Voices from places not explored.

On distant shores, where waters gleam,
Stories weave through time's embrace.
In every wave, a hopeful dream,
A chorus sung, a timeless grace.

From hills where wildflowers bloom,
To valleys deep, where shadows play,
Each note dissolves the night's dark gloom,
As memories dance in bright array.

In twilight's arms, they call to me,
With melodies both soft and grand.
Each voice a thread, a mystery,
Stitched in love by fate's own hand.

So heed the whispers on the air,
For every song has truth to guide.
In voices from afar, I dare,
To find the light where dreams abide.

Ascending Through the Ash

From embers low, a spark ignites,
A phoenix dreams of skies anew.
With every breath, the darkness fights,
And rises with a vibrant hue.

Through shadows thick, the spirit soars,
Casting off the weight of pain.
A journey forged through opened doors,
Emerging strong from fiery rain.

The past may linger, but I rise,
With every trial, I am reborn.
Eyes set toward the open skies,
With hopes that flicker like the dawn.

So let the ashes fall away,
Their whispers become distant dust.
I'll find my path; I'll find my way,
With faith that binds my heart in trust.

In soaring heights, my spirit sings,
A song of growth, a life anew.
From the depths, I'll spread my wings,
Ascending through the ash, I flew.

Fragments Left Behind

In the dust of memories lost,
Whispers float, a gentle frost.
Scattered dreams like autumn leaves,
Time unfolds as the heart believes.

Echoes dance in quiet rooms,
Laughter fades, yet silence blooms.
Photographs, a fleeting glance,
Capture moments, a wistful dance.

Beneath the ashes, embers glow,
Stories linger, always flow.
Pieces of us in shadows lie,
Tales of love that never die.

Upon the paths we did not take,
Regrets linger, softly ache.
Yet in sorrow, there's a grace,
Within the void, a sacred space.

Each fragment tells a tale unique,
In brokenness, the soul will speak.
In the quiet, we find our way,
Through shattered moments, we will stay.

Unraveled Threads of Time

Threads once woven, now unwind,
In the fabric of our mind.
Moments stitched with hopes and dreams,
Frayed edges tell of silent screams.

In the loom of memories bright,
Colors fade into the night.
What was whole is now askew,
A tapestry of me and you.

Time slips softly, like a sigh,
Promises lost, a distant cry.
Yet within the twists and bends,
A notion that the journey mends.

With every knot, a lesson learned,
In the chaos, wisdom earned.
Though frayed, these threads still bind,
A journey mapped within the mind.

As the clock continues to chime,
We find beauty in the grime.
Unraveled yet, we stand aligned,
In the web of love entwined.

Glimmers of Hope Ahead

In the dawn's embrace, we rise,
Softly painted in the skies.
Light spills gold on weary souls,
Awakening the heart it holds.

Through the valleys, shadows creep,
Yet in silence, dreams will leap.
Resilience whispers on the breeze,
Encouraging the spirit's ease.

With every step, a chance unfolds,
Stories waiting to be told.
Casting doubts into the night,
Chasing paths towards the light.

Hope shines bright like morning dew,
Embracing all that we pursue.
In the struggle, strength is found,
In the noise, a steady sound.

So we journey, hearts afire,
Climbing mountains, reaching higher.
For within us, the power lies,
To find our wings and touch the skies.

Whirlwinds of Change

In the tempest, we are spun,
Life's mosaic has begun.
Fleeting moments, ever strange,
Caught within the whirlwinds' change.

Paths diverging like the sea,
What was once is yet to be.
Dreams like leaves in sudden gusts,
Ride the storms, ignite the dust.

Through the chaos, voices rise,
Chanting truths beneath the skies.
In the echoes, courage calls,
As the dauntless spirit falls.

Change is but a dance of fate,
Every choice we give a weight.
With every turn, a brand new hue,
Painting life with visions true.

Embrace the winds that shape our way,
Through night's cloak and light of day.
For in the heart of every breeze,
Lies the power to believe.